THE OFFICIAL
EVERTON FOOTBALL CLUB
ANNUAL 2018

Written by Darren Griffiths, Adam Clark and Howard Frost

Designed by Lucy Boyd

A Grange Publication

© 2017. Published by Grange Communications Ltd., Edinburgh, under licence from Everton Football Club.

Printed in the EU.

Photographs © Everton Football Club.

ISBN 978-1-911287-70-4

CONTENTS

RONALD
KOEMAN

RONALD KOEMAN WAS A WORLD SUPERSTAR AS A PLAYER. THE EVERTON MANAGER PLAYED FOR SOME OF THE BIGGEST TEAMS IN EUROPE AND WAS A EUROPEAN CHAMPIONSHIP WINNER WITH HOLLAND IN 1988. HERE'S TWENTY FACTS THAT PERHAPS YOU DIDN'T KNOW ABOUT THE BOSS...

1. Ronald and his brother Erwin were both born in the city of Zaandam in Holland. Zaandam is famous for being the first ever European city to have a McDonald's!

2. When Ronald made his professional debut for FC Groningen at the age of 17 he was the third youngest player in the club's history.

3. Even though he was a defender, he scored 33 goals in his first three seasons.

4. In 1983 Ronald made his international debut for Holland. Erwin made his own debut in the same game.

5. Like Everton, Ronald won a league title in 1984/85. He was with Ajax and they won the Dutch First Division (the Eredivisie).

6. Whilst at Ajax, Ronald had the legendary Johan Cruyff as his manager.

7. In 1988 he helped PSV Eindhoven to win their one and only European Cup, scoring one of the penalties in a 5-4 shoot-out victory against Benfica.

8. Amazingly, Ronald scored 21 league goals in that 1987/88 season that saw PSV win the Dutch title and the Dutch Cup as well as the European Cup.

9. To cap a memorable season, Ronald won the 1988 European Championships with Holland, beating Russia in the final.

10. In 1989 Ronald teamed up again with Cruyff when the great man signed him for Barcelona.

11. One of his team-mates at the Nou Camp was current Manchester City manager, Pep Guardiola.

12. In 1991 when Barcelona lost in the European Cup Winners' Cup final against Manchester United, Ronald scored their goal in a 2-1 defeat.

13. In 1992, Ronald won the European Cup for Barcelona with the only goal of a 1-0 win in the final against Sampdoria at Wembley.

14. In 1993/94 Barcelona lost in the final of the Champions League against AC Milan but Ronald ended the season as joint top-scorer in the competition with eight goals...as a defender!

15. Ronald holds the La Liga record for consecutively converted penalties – scoring 25 on the run without missing.

16. His 239 career goals make him the highest scoring defender in history.

17. Only Lionel Messi has scored more goals from direct free-kicks for Barcelona than Ronald.

18. After retiring he was part of the Holland coaching staff at the 1998 World Cup, where they lost to Argentina in the quarter-finals.

19. Ronald has since managed the 'Big 3' teams in Holland – Ajax, PSV and Feyenoord.

20. His first job in England was with Southampton where he won the Premier League Manager of the Month three times.

WE ARE THE CHAMPIONS!

Did you know Everton are the reigning Premier League champions?

Premier League 2 that is!

It's the competition for all the best Under-23s teams in England and, in 2016/17, the Blues finished top of the pile, ahead of the likes of Manchester City, Liverpool and Chelsea.

In total, our Under-23s – coached by former Blues defender David Unsworth – won 15 of their 22 games, losing just four times all season!

The top scorer was midfielder Harry Charsley with seven goals and there were some very familiar names among his teammates, too!

Tom Davies, Mason Holgate, Ademola Lookman and Dominic Calvert-Lewin all ended up with winners' medals, while Jonjoe Kenny was the team's captain and got to lift the trophy at Goodison Park after their final game of the season against... Liverpool!

What an achievement!

BLUES WIN THE WORLD CUP!

Okay, so they didn't do it on their own, but it's true... **FIVE** Everton players helped England Under-20s win the biggest tournament of them all in June, the World Cup!

Dominic Calvert-Lewin, Callum Connolly, Kieran Dowell, Jonjoe Kenny and Ademola Lookman all played their part as the Young Lions, managed by former Manchester City winger Paul Simpson, battled their way to glory.

And that's not all... Calvert-Lewin was the hero in the final, slotting home the only goal as England beat South American country Venezuela 1-0!

The tournament was held in South Korea in Asia and it was the first time any England side had reached a World Cup final since the senior team famously lifted the World Cup at Wembley all the way back in 1966!

On their way to the final, England defeated Argentina, hosts South Korea, Costa Rica, Mexico and the much-fancied Azzurrini of Italy!

Well done, boys!

JULES RIMET FOR RAY

This is left-back Ray Wilson, the only man to win the senior World Cup while playing for Everton!

He was a key part of the England side in 1966, when the Three Lions overcame West Germany 4-2 in the final thanks to a hat-trick from striker Geoff Hurst and a man of the match performance from future Everton star Alan Ball!

The trophy England won was called the 'Jules Rimet', named after the FIFA president who passed a vote that led to the very first World Cup taking place in Uruguay in 1930.

Four months before the tournament in 1966, the Jules Rimet trophy was stolen from an exhibition at Westminster Central Hall in London, only to be found again seven days later by a heroic dog named Pickles!

UNDER-20 WORLD CUP VITAL STATS

ENGLAND TOTAL MATCHES: 7
ENGLAND TOTAL GOALS: 12
GOALS BY EVERTON PLAYERS: 6
ASSISTS BY EVERTON PLAYERS: 6

WAYNE ROONEY

When Wayne Rooney scored the winning goal for Everton against Portsmouth on 13 March 2004, little did he know that it would be an incredible 4,900 days before he scored for the club again at Goodison Park. Of course, in between he became Manchester United's all-time record goalscorer and gained winners' medals in the Champions League, Premier League, FA Cup and League Cup.

But in July 2017 he came home! Evertonians rejoiced when he put pen to paper on a deal with the Toffees that brought him back to his beloved Goodison Park.

And as for Wayne Rooney himself, he was just as pleased....

What's it like for your family and friends to see you back in an Everton jersey?

They're all made up. Everyone supported me when I went to United, but now they can support me and the Everton team! My dad came to watch me in Manchester and now he will only have a five minutes drive to watch me again so he is really happy! Everyone is delighted I've come back but, again, I've come back to win things with Everton, not for the sentiment.

It's clear how much Everton still means to you.

As a baby and all through my life I've been an Everton fan. That's not changed. Obviously, football now is more like a job and sometimes you move on to different things, which I did, but in terms of being a fan, I've always been a fan of Everton Football Club. Once the opportunity arose to come back here, I was delighted.

Although you won all those trophies and broke records with Man United and England, were you nervous when you first came back to Everton?

No, I was just excited to get in, meet the lads and get started. I wasn't driving in with a nervous feeling, I was just excited and couldn't wait to get going. Once I knew Ronald was interested in me it was a no-brainer to come back. There were other options but this was the only place I was going to play football.

Was it strange to hear your name being chanted again at your beloved Goodison Park?

Yes, of course. But the fans have been great and the reception I have had since I have been back has been incredible. Hopefully I can repay that with good performances and goals and trying to help the team win. It's great for me to be back at Goodison and playing in front of the home fans.

When you left Goodison you were a teenager but now you're a senior professional. Do you enjoy giving the younger lads some advice?

Yes, I do but obviously I have to concentrate on playing and training too. Of course, there's things I can help players with, especially the younger ones but I have to keep doing my best in training and in the games and that's the way to set a good example to the other players.

When you rejoined you said winning a trophy with Everton would be the best moment of your career. With everything you've achieved, explain why that would mean so much?

To win a trophy at a club you've grown up supporting would be great. The last time we won something was in 1995 so to bring some silverware back to Goodison would be up there. It would mean a lot to me and the fans.

It was 4,900 days between your last goal for Everton and the winner you scored against Stoke City at the start of this season. Your celebration told the world just how much it meant to you...

It was a special moment for me. On a personal note, I am absolutely delighted. It was a lot of relief and emotion coming out. I've felt at home since my first day back at the training ground. I had been looking forward to that day for a long time and thankfully it was a good day.

Answers on p60-61

WAYNE ROONEY QUIZ

1. At the start of the season, who was the only player to have scored more Premier League goals than Wayne?

A) Alan Shearer   B) Cristiano Ronaldo   C) Thierry Henry

2. Wayne once scored an overhead kick that was voted as the Goal of the Season. Who was it against?

A) Liverpool   B) Manchester City   C) Arsenal

3. Wayne played in the 2002 FA Youth Cup final for Everton against which team?

A) Ipswich Town   B) Aston Villa   C) West Ham

4. When Wayne made his England debut at just 17 years old, who was the England manager?

A) Kevin Keegan   B) Glenn Hoddle   C) Sven-Goran Eriksson

5. Wayne's first major international tournament was the 2004 European Championships. In four games how many goals did he score?

A) Two   B) Three   C) Four

THE FIRST TIME AROUND!

THE STORY OF WAYNE ROONEY'S FIRST SPELL AT EVERTON...

After making his debut in August 2002, Wayne Rooney played 77 games and scored 18 goals for Everton before joining Manchester United in the summer of 2004. Almost exactly 13 years later, he came home again! Here are some of the highlights of his first spell with the Blues...

1 During his first spell with the Blues, Wayne didn't score a Merseyside derby goal ... but that didn't stop him getting involved when tempers flared!

2 17 August 2002 - Wayne makes his senior professional debut against Tottenham Hotspur at Goodison Park.

3 1 October 2002 - Still aged just 16, he scores his first ever goals, netting twice in a 3-0 League Cup win away to Wrexham.

4 19 October 2002 - Remember the Name! Kevin Campbell gives a piggy-back to the boy who has just scored his first ever Premier League goal - a 25-yard screamer against Arsenal.

5 26 April 2002 - Wayne smashes home a 92nd minute winner to give Everton a dramatic 2-1 victory against Aston Villa at Goodison.

6 3 November 2002 - Everton hadn't won away at Leeds United for over 50 years ... until Wayne celebrated his recent 18th birthday with the only goal of the game!

7 26 December 2002 - An unhappy Christmas for Wayne as he picks up his first ever red card away to Birmingham City on Boxing Day.

8 12 February 2003 - Wayne becomes England's youngest ever full international when Australia are the visitors to West Ham's Upton Park.

9 6 April 2003 - Wayne opens the scoring against Newcastle United at Goodison.

10 26 July 2003 - Whoops! Wayne goes a bit close to the bone with his summer haircut for a friendly at Glasgow Rangers.

11 26 December 2003 - Wayne didn't do much defending in those days but he wasn't the only player who failed to stop Cristiano Ronaldo in his tracks!

12 21 February 2004 - The only time Wayne scored twice in one game in the Premier League for Everton was against Southampton at St Mary's.

PLAYER PROFILES

1 GOALKEEPER

JORDAN PICKFORD
DOB: 7 March 1994
Joined Everton: June 2017
Past clubs: Sunderland (2011-2017)
FACT When Jordan signed for Everton, he became the most expensive British goalkeeper of all time!

33 GOALKEEPER

JOEL ROBLES
DOB: 17 June 1990
Joined Everton: July 2013
Past clubs: Atletico Madrid (2009-2013), Wigan Athletic (2012-2013, Loan)
FACT Joel won the FA Cup in 2013 while on loan at Wigan from Atletico Madrid!

22 GOALKEEPER

5 DEFENDER

MAARTEN STEKELENBURG
DOB: 22 September 1982
Joined Everton: July 2016
Past clubs: Ajax (2002-2011), Roma (2011-2013), Fulham (2013-2016)
FACT Maarten played in goal for Holland in the 2010 World Cup final in South Africa! Sadly, the Dutch were beaten 1-0 by Spain.

ASHLEY WILLIAMS
DOB: 23 August 1984
Joined Everton: August 2016
Past clubs: Hednesford Town (2001-2003), Stockport County (2003-2008), Swansea City (2008-2016)
FACT Before becoming a footballer, Ashley worked as a waiter in a restaurant and on the coconut shy at a theme park!

23 DEFENDER

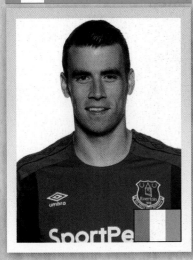

SEAMUS COLEMAN

DOB: 11 October 1988

Joined Everton: January 2009

Past clubs: Sligo Rovers (2006-2009)

FACT Seamus used to play Gaelic football – a cross between football and rugby that is popular in Ireland!

25 DEFENDER

RAMIRO FUNES MORI

DOB: 5 March 1991

Joined Everton: September 2015

Past clubs: River Plate (2011-2015)

FACT Ramiro has an identical twin brother, Rogelio, who has played for the Argentina national team as a striker!

30 DEFENDER

MASON HOLGATE

DOB: 22 October 1996

Joined Everton: August 2015

Past clubs: Barnsley (2014-2015)

FACT Mason was part of the England Under-21s squad at last summer's European Championships in Poland!

15 DEFENDER

CUCO MARTINA

DOB: 25 September 1989

Joined Everton: July 2017

Past clubs: RBC Roosendaal (2008-2011), RKC Waalwijk (2011-2013), Twente (2013-2015), Southampton (2015-2017)

FACT Cuco is captain of Curaçao, an island of around 160,000 people, which is 4,600 miles away in the Caribbean!

4 DEFENDER

MICHAEL KEANE

DOB: 11 January 1993

Nationality: English

Past clubs: Manchester United (2011-2015), Burnley (2015-2017)

FACT Along with Paul Pogba, Jesse Lingard and brother Will, Michael was part of the Manchester United team that won the FA Youth Cup in 2011.

PLAYER PROFILES

3 DEFENDER

LEIGHTON BAINES

DOB: 11 December 1984

Joined Everton: August 2007

Past clubs: Wigan Athletic (2002-2007)

FACT Leighton has twice been named in the PFA Premier League Team of the Year, in both 2011/12 and 2012/13!

6 DEFENDER

PHIL JAGIELKA

DOB: 17 August 1982

Joined Everton: July 2007

Past clubs: Sheffield United (2000-2007)

FACT During his time at Sheffield United, 'Jags' ended up playing in goal on FOUR different occasions!

8 MIDFIELDER

ROSS BARKLEY

DOB: 5 December 1993

Joined Everton: 2005 (Aged 11)

Past clubs: None

FACT Before making it in the first team, big Everton fan Ross used to be a ball boy at Goodison Park!

18 MIDFIELDER

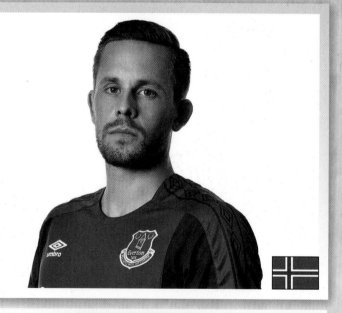

GYLFI SIGURDSSON

DOB: 8 September 1989

Nationality: Icelandic

Joined Everton: August 2017

Past clubs: Reading (2008-2010), Hoffenheim (2010-2012), Tottenham Hotspur (2012-2014), Swansea City (2014-2017)

FACT Gylfi's very cool middle name is Thor! Gylfi is a very good golfer and plays off a handicap of just four.

17 MIDFIELDER

IDRISSA GANA GUEYE

DOB: 26 September 1989

Joined Everton: August 2016

Past clubs: Lille (2010-2015), Aston Villa (2015-2016)

FACT Gana made 135 Premier League tackles last season – more than any other player!

2 MIDFIELDER

MORGAN SCHNEIDERLIN

DOB: 8 November 1989

Joined Everton: January 2017

Past clubs: Strasbourg (2006-2008), Southampton (2008-2015), Manchester United (2015-2017)

FACT Morgan has represented France at every level from Under-16s upwards and was part of the senior squad that reached the final of Euro 2016!

21 MIDFIELDER

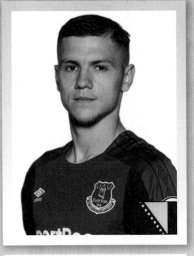

MUHAMED BESIC

DOB: 10 September 1992

Joined Everton: July 2014

Past clubs: Hamburg (2010-2012), Ferencvaros (2012-2014)

FACT Although he plays for Bosnia, Mo was born and brought up in Berlin, Germany!

26 MIDFIELDER

TOM DAVIES

DOB: 30 June 1998

Joined Everton: 2009 (Aged 11)

Past clubs: None

FACT Tom's uncle, Alan Whittle, was part of the Everton team that were crowned champions of England in 1969/70!

PLAYER PROFILES

27 MIDFIELDER

NIKOLA VLASIC

DOB: 4 October 1997

Joined Everton: August 2017

Past clubs: Hajduk Split (2010-2014)

FACT Nikola's sister, Blanka, is a two-times high jump world champion who has also claimed silver and bronze medals for Croatia at the Olympic Games!

12 MIDFIELDER

AARON LENNON

DOB: 16 April 1987

Joined Everton: February 2015 (initially on loan)

Past clubs: Leeds United (2003-2005), Tottenham Hotspur (2005-2015)

FACT As a youngster, Aaron represented Yorkshire as a 100m sprinter!

16 MIDFIELDER

JAMES McCARTHY

DOB: 12 November 1990

Joined Everton: September 2013

Past clubs: Hamilton Academical (2006-2009), Wigan Athletic (2009-2013)

FACT James made his senior debut for Hamilton Academical when he was aged just 15!

31 FORWARD

ADEMOLA LOOKMAN

DOB: 20 October 1997

Joined Everton: January 2017

Past clubs: Charlton Athletic (2015-2017)

FACT London-born Ademola achieved three A*s and five As in his GCSEs!

10 FORWARD

WAYNE ROONEY
DOB: 24 October 1985

Joined Everton: July 2017

Past clubs: Everton (2002-2004), Manchester United (2004-2017)

FACT Wayne is both Manchester United's and England's record goalscorer. He re-joined Everton in the summer having scored 253 times in 559 appearances for the Red Devils. Impressive!

11 FORWARD

KEVIN MIRALLAS

DOB: 5 October 1987

Joined Everton: August 2012

Past clubs: Lille (2004-2008), Saint-Etienne (2008-2010), Olympiacos (2010-2012)

FACT Kevin's full name is Kevin Antonio Joel Gislain Mirallas y Castillo!

20 FORWARD

DAVY KLAASSEN

DOB: 21 February 1993

Joined Everton: June 2017

Past clubs: Ajax (2011-2017)

FACT Aged 18, Davy scored on his league debut for Ajax... just 42 seconds after coming on!

9 FORWARD

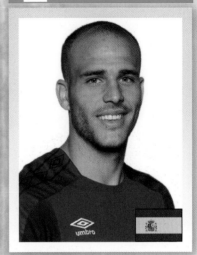

SANDRO RAMIREZ

DOB: 9 July 1995

Joined Everton: July 2018

Past clubs: Barcelona (2014-2016), Malaga (2016-2017)

FACT When he's not playing football, Sandro has a passion for scuba diving!

7 FORWARD

YANNICK BOLASIE

DOB: 24 May 1989

Joined Everton: August 2016

Past clubs: Hillingdon Borough (2006-2007), Floriana (2007-2008), Plymouth Argyle (2008-2011), Bristol City (2011-2012), Crystal Palace (2012-2016)

FACT Yannick had an agreement with first club Hillingdon that they would buy him a burger for every goal he scored. He got EIGHT in one game!

29 FORWARD

DOMINIC CALVERT-LEWIN

DOB: 16 March 1997

Joined Everton: August 2016

Past clubs: Sheffield United (2014-2016)

FACT Dominic scored the winning goal for England in the 2017 Under-20s World Cup final!

MY FOOTBALL HERO

MORGAN SCHNEIDERLIN HERO: ZINEDINE ZIDANE

HERO FACTFILE:
DOB: 23 June 1972
Position: Midfielder
Nationality: French
Caps (Goals): 108 (31)
Played for: Cannes (1989-1992), Bordeaux (1992-1996), Juventus (1996-2001), Real Madrid (2001-2006)

CAREER IN BRIEF
Considered one of the greatest midfielders of all time, Zidane won 13 leagues and cups during his club career and also tasted World Cup and European Championship glory with France. He is now a manager and led Real Madrid to their second successive Champions League title last season!

MORGAN SAYS:
"He was an amazing player – his class and technique on the pitch were a joy to watch. For me, he was the best player ever!"

MASON HOLGATE   HERO: RIO FERDINAND

HERO FACTFILE:
DOB: 7 November 1978
Position: Defender
Nationality: English
Caps (Goals): 81 (3)
Played for: West Ham United (1996-2000), Leeds United (2000-2002), Manchester United (2002-2014), QPR (2014-15)

CAREER IN BRIEF
One of the most successful defenders ever to play in the Premier League, Ferdinand won 11 major honours and featured in three England World Cup squads. Named in the PFA Premier League team of the year on six occasions, he became the most expensive defender in history when he moved to Leeds United in 2000, and again when he joined Manchester United two years later!

MASON SAYS:
"He was someone I admired a lot as a player, and growing up I tried to base my game on what he would do."

YANNICK BOLASIE   HERO: THIERRY HENRY

HERO FACTFILE:
DOB: 17 August 1977
Position: Striker
Nationality: French
Caps (Goals): 123 (51)
Played for: Monaco (1994-1999), Juventus (1999), Arsenal (1999-2007), Barcelona (2007-2010), New York Red Bulls (2010-2014)

CAREER IN BRIEF
A World Cup and European Championship winner with France, Henry is the fifth highest scorer in Premier League history, having netted 175 goals in just 258 games. All of those came at Arsenal, where he won two titles and two FA Cups, before he went on to scoop another five major trophies with Barcelona!

YANNICK SAYS:
"He was a goalscorer but he also had loads of flair and loved to take players on. I liked that about him."

Everybody has a football hero - even footballers themselves!
We asked some of the players to reveal who it was they admired
when growing up - and why...

PHIL JAGIELKA

HERO: STEVE JAGIELKA

HERO FACTFILE:
DOB: 10 March 1978
Position: Midfielder
Nationality: English
Played for: Stoke City
(1996-1997), Shrewsbury
Town (1997-2004), Accrington
Stanley (2004-2006),
Droylsden (2006-2007),
Telford United (2007-2009),
Hednesford Town (2009-2012)

CAREER IN BRIEF
A midfielder who loved a tackle, Steve is
Phil's older brother! Despite starting his
career with Stoke City, he is most fondly
remembered by fans of Shrewsbury
Town, where he made 197 appearances
and scored 20 goals. He would later go
on to win the National Conference (now
the National League) with Accrington
Stanley, helping the club climb back into
the Football League!

PHIL SAYS:
"Being the youngest of the family, you look up to what your big brother is doing. I was always following him around and wanting to play football like him."

TOM DAVIES

HERO: MIKEL ARTETA

HERO FACTFILE:
DOB: 26 March 1982
Position: Midfielder
Nationality: Spanish
Played for: Barcelona
B (1999-2002), Rangers
(2002-2004), Real
Socieded (2004-2005),
Everton (2005-2011),
Arsenal (2011-2016)

CAREER IN BRIEF
One of the most skilful players to pull on
the Everton shirt in the Premier League
era, Arteta wowed Blues fans during
a six-year spell at the Club, scoring 34
goals in 209 appearances. Remarkably,
he never got a cap for Spain but did
go on to win two FA Cups with Arsenal
before retiring and becoming a coach to
Pep Guardiola at Manchester City.

TOM SAYS:
"He was just quality in our midfield playing alongside Tim Cahill. Watching him made me realise that playing for Everton was what I wanted to do one day."

KEVIN MIRALLAS   HERO: MATTHEW LE TISSIER

HERO FACTFILE:
DOB: 14 October 1968
Position: Midfielder
Nationality: English
Caps (Goals): 8 (0)
Played for:
Southampton (1986-
2002), Eastleigh (2002-
2003)

CAREER IN BRIEF
Nicknamed 'Le God' by Southampton
fans, Le Tissier was famous for trying
what other footballers wouldn't. With
a bagful of skills and tricks, and a
brilliant habit of scoring long-range
goals, particularly volleys, he was
one of the Premier League's earliest
entertainers! That he got ONLY eight
England caps is still questioned by
Three Lions fans today!

KEVIN SAYS:
"I always used to look out for him when I started watching the Premier League. Some of the goals he scored were just outrageous!"

A YEAR IN PICTURES: YANNICK

1
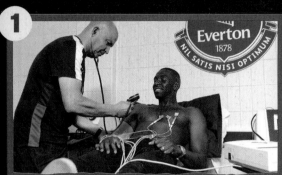
Yannick's year at Everton started with his medical at Finch Farm....which he passed with flying colours!

2

...then he had to meet the media to explain why he swapped Crystal Palace for Everton.

3

..Yannick was one of the first studio guests of the season on the Everton TV Show. He joined Ian Snodin on the sofa for the hour-long programme.

4

...He quickly got into the swing of things by attending an Everton in the Community Kicks Session where he took on some martial arts lessons.

5

...and also showed the participants of the value of a proper warm up. At least, we think that's what he's doing!

6

...He had to smarten himself up considerably for the special 'Cocktails & Canapes' event that took place in Liverpool city centre.

7

...there are and messages to

10

...When we invited some of the players to a graffitti centre, guess who was first to volunteer!

11
...and he certainly looked at home!

12
..there u USM Finch crazy golf with Ja

...iews to do
...M Finch Farm.

8

...then it was back to more casual attire when he joined Dominic Calvert-Lewin at a Liverpool restaurant for some cookery lessons!

9

...Wonder whose dish tasted the best?!

...f sport at
...Yannick played
...and Tom Cleverley.

13

...Yannick was happy to mingle with supporters on the Blue Carpet before the Everton End of Season Awards evening.

14

ELEBRATION EVENING

At the very end of the season, Yannick travelled to London to present former Manchester United striker Andy Cole with a special award.

INTERNATIONAL BLUES!

How well do you know where your Everton heroes come from?
We've highlighted NINE countries on the map of Europe below –
but can you link each player to the country they play for?
Take a point for each you get right! We've started you off by
doing the first one for you...

KEVIN MIRALLAS

MUHAMED BESIC

SANDRO RAMIREZ

MORGAN SCHNEIDERLIN

DAVY KLAASSEN

ROSS BARKLEY

ASHLEY WILLIAMS

SEAMUS COLEMAN

GYLFI SIGURDSSON

ICELAND

HINT
If you need a bit of help, check out our player profiles starting on page 12!

REPUBLIC OF IRELAND

WALES

ENGLAND

HOLLAND

BELGIUM

FRANCE

BOSNIA

SPAIN

Answers on p60-61

TWENTY THINGS YOU DIDN'T KNOW ABOUT...
MICHAEL KEANE

1. He was born in Stockport on 11 January 1993, which makes him a Capricorn.

2. His twin brother Will plays for Hull City.

3. He is 6' 3" tall.

4. Michael joined Manchester United's Academy at the age of 16 in 2009.

5. He signed his first professional contract at Old Trafford on his 18th birthday.

6. He made his United first-team debut in the League Cup on 25 October 2011, coming on as a substitute in the 70th minute of a 4th round victory over Aldershot Town.

7. Also making a sub appearance for United that night was a teenage Paul Pogba!

8. In 2012 Michael was named as Manchester United's Reserve Team Player of the Year.

9. He also picked up a Reserve League winners medal that year.

10. Whilst at United, Michael had loan spells with Leicester City, Derby County, Blackburn Rovers and Burnley.

11. On 12 February 2013, he scored his first ever senior goal. It was for Leicester City against Huddersfield Town in an FA Cup match.

12. His final loan spell at Burnley was made permanent in January 2015 when he signed a three-and-a-half year deal for an undisclosed fee.

13. In 2016 he helped Burnley win the Championship.

14. Michael was one of four Burnley players in the PFA Championship Team of the Year, alongside Tom Heaton, Joey Barton and Andre Gray.

15. In April 2017 he was one of the six nominees for the PFA Young Player of the Season.

16. Keane has Irish ancestors and played Under-17 and Under-19 international football for the Republic of Ireland.

17. He switched his allegiance to England in 2012 and made his Under-19 debut in a 5-0 win against Slovakia.

18. His twin brother was an England team-mate that night and he scored two goals.

19. He helped England U-19s reach the semi-finals of the 2012 European Championships and the following March he made his Under-21 debut.

20. On 22 March 2017 Michael made his senior England debut in a defeat against Germany, when Lukas Podolski ended his international career by scoring the only goal of the game.

JORDAN PICKFORD
– MY FIRST

The Blues shot-stopper gets his thinking cap on to recall his first...

Car...
I treated myself to an Audi A3 when I passed my test. It was a decent car and they're good memories, getting out on the road for the first time.

Football memory...
I always used to go and watch my brother's team back home in Washington and one day there was another game taking place on the next pitch. I just joined in, got thrown in at the deep end and ended up in goal. That was the start of me playing for them and how I became a keeper!

Birthday present...
My mam and dad always tried to spoil us to be honest but it was probably a pair of football boots!

Holiday...
My mam and dad got married in the Dominican Republic and I hated it. I was only two or three at the time and apparently I just cried the whole time. It must've been too hot for me!

Football hero...
I've always said there's two. One is Peter Schmeichel, because he was at his peak when I was growing up and starting to watch football on the tv. Then, as a Sunderland fan, it's got to be Tommy Sørensen for saving Alan Shearer's penalty and helping us to a win at St James' Park in 2000.

Pet...
It was my dog, a little Jack Russell called Molly.

Album...
I can't remember. It would have been some sort of rave music, though!

Mentor...
It's got to be Mark Prudhoe. Going in to Sunderland at eight or nine years of age, he was my first keeper coach. He left the club but came back and helped me develop later on in my time there as well.

Roommate...
He wasn't necessarily my first but in the last couple of seasons for England Under-21s it's been Duncan Watmore, my teammate from Sunderland. We had a good craic playing Rory McIlroy PGA Tour on the Xbox. I'd batter him as well!

Shirt swap...
It was at the Under-17 World Cup in Mexico and I swapped with one of the German keepers. We got beat in the quarter-finals but I've still got it. It's at my mam's house somewhere!

Initiation song...
That was in South Korea with Sunderland as a young lad. I got summoned up and I was a bit nervous like. I did *Not Nineteen Forever* by The Courteeners. It wasn't the best but it is what it is. It's one of those things you just have to get through!

Football rollicking....
I've had plenty! Kevin Ball at Sunderland always used to give us a few but it was always for the best and to make me a better person and a better goalkeeper.

NIKOLA VLASIC

Just as the summer transfer window closed, Everton swooped in to sign a player who had already played against us twice in the previous two weeks! Nikola Vlasic joined the Blues on deadline day from our Europa League opponents Hajduk Split...

How pleased are you to become an Everton player?
I am very excited to play for this big club. It is a big honour for me and I know how big Everton is. I also know the big names, the big stars that came this summer, players like Gylfi Sigurdsson, Wayne Rooney, Michael Keane, Jordan Pickford and more. I am very excited to play with the guys. Of course, the manager is a big name in football as well. I think it will be very good here. There is no measure for how much they can improve me. I want to learn from them and become a better player and person. These players have already done things in life that I want to achieve. It is a very big plus.

Was it strange to join Everton so soon after playing against us in the Europa League?
After the first leg of the Europa League game, I heard that some journalists from England were pleased with my game. Then, after the second game in Split, there was something concrete there and I was very proud when I heard about it. There were some other clubs interested but Everton was the biggest club and I wanted to come here.

When I came to Everton with Hajduk Split we learned it was one of the oldest stadiums in the country. In Croatia, there is distance between the fans and the pitch but at Goodison Park, the fans are so close and it's perfect. The passion that I felt from Everton was so warm.

How much of an influence was Ronald Koeman in your decision?
When there is a manager like Ronald Koeman who wants you, there is no need to talk about it much. I wanted to come here, because of the manager, because of the big players, because of the reputation of the Club. It is the opportunity of a lifetime.

Have you always wanted to play in the English Premier League?
The Premier League is the best league in the world and it is such a big honour for me to be here. When I heard that Everton were interested in me, I just knew I wanted to come here straight away. I only saw Everton, then. Whenever someone called my manager or my father, I told them I only wanted to come to Everton.

I started playing first-team football in Croatia from a very young age. There were ups and downs but I'm very happy to be in this place and I'm very thankful. I have already played a lot of games but the Premier League is something else. Playing football in England is a much bigger stage - football is number one here.

How would you describe your style of play?
I'm a guy who likes to play with the ball at his feet. I do a lot of movement and dribbling with the ball. I like to play in the middle. I think the fans will enjoy my style of play.

The ambition of the Club is to ultimately play in the Champions League and I want to help achieve that goal. I believe in myself and in this team - I think we can do great things together.

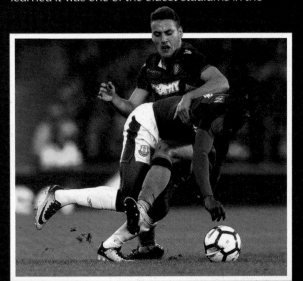

OLD STADIUM QUIZ

You'll probably need the help of a grown-up to get these answers right! Here are nine photographs of old football grounds that Everton have played at but that no longer exist. See if you can identify them from the pictures and the clues provided...

This team that used to play at this stadium started the 2017/18 season in League Two.

A

Everton played a few FA Cup semi-finals here before the team moved to the Commonwealth games stadium in 2002.

B

Gary Lineker scored loads of goals at this stadium but the team had moved by the time they won the Premier League!

C

Everton suffered a shock FA Cup defeat here in 2003 when the home team were 92nd in the Football League!

D

This place had a famous 'roar' before the team moved a new ground that shares its name with Benfica's stadium.

E

Everton won the 1984 FA Cup semi-final here and Alan Ball played here for a while.

F

There will be no more blowing bubbles at this stadium after it closed in 2016.

G

This was home to the Crazy Gang in the 1980s!

H

This little ground on the south coast was replaced by St Mary's.

I

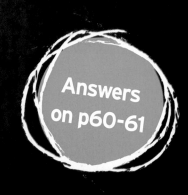

Answers on p60-61

GYLFI SIGURDSSON

The summer of 2017 saw Everton break a club transfer record when Gylfi Sigurdsson joined us. The Icelandic international has plenty of Premier League experience with Tottenham Hotspur and Swansea City and he's now hoping to make a name for himself as a Toffee!

WHAT ARE YOUR AIMS AT EVERTON?
I would like to score as many goals as possible and create as many goals for my team mates as I can. But it is always the same thing. As long as the team is winning I will be more than happy.

WE'VE CHECKED YOUR STATS FOR THE 2016/17 SEASON AND NOT MANY PREMIER LEAGUE PLAYERS RAN FURTHER THAN YOU!
Swansea had to defend for long periods, especially in the first part of last season. That was one of the reasons I was up there. Another was I was very lucky with injuries - I played every game. But I do try to work hard for the team and I think that suits the pressing game the manager wants.

WAS IT GOOD TO BE ABLE TO PLAY ALONGSIDE WAYNE ROONEY FOR THE FIRST TIME?
Yes, of course and hopefully, we can work well together. He is obviously a player who was fantastic for Everton in the short period of time before he went to United and he will be again the second time

around. And everyone knows his history, how well he has done for his country and for Manchester United, so hopefully he will continue the goalscoring form he has shown for the past 10 or 15 years and that will suit the team.

DID THE BIG TRANSFER FEE THAT EVERTON PAID BOTHER YOU?
It is not something I am interested in or focused on. It is out of my hands, it is nothing to do with me. But I think it shows the intent and how much the manager wanted me.

YOU PLAYED WITH ASHLEY WILLIAMS AT SWANSEA CITY...DID HE CONVINCE YOU TO COME AND JOIN HIM HERE AT EVERTON?
Yes, I spoke to Ash. He wasn't at Swansea last season but he was the year before. I did speak to him last season and during this season about how it was up here and he told me it was a fantastic club and I think it is. I am delighted to be here.

YOU ARE A SET-PIECE EXPERT SO DOES THAT MEAN THE EVERTON GOALIES WILL HAVE TO DO EXTRA WORK TO HELP YOU PRACTICE?
I think it is up to them if they want to stay out! But, yes of course I do like to practice them. It is something I enjoy and I am sure the keepers will be happy to help out!

CAN WE NOW EXPECT LOTS OF SUPPORTERS FROM ICELAND TO MAKE EVERTON THEIR NUMBER ONE PREMIER LEAGUE TEAM?
Well I think it will be easier for them to watch me. It is quite handy to fly to Manchester then drive across for the games. Previously, people had to fly into London then drive to Swansea, so I am sure there will be people here at Christmas, coming to the big games.

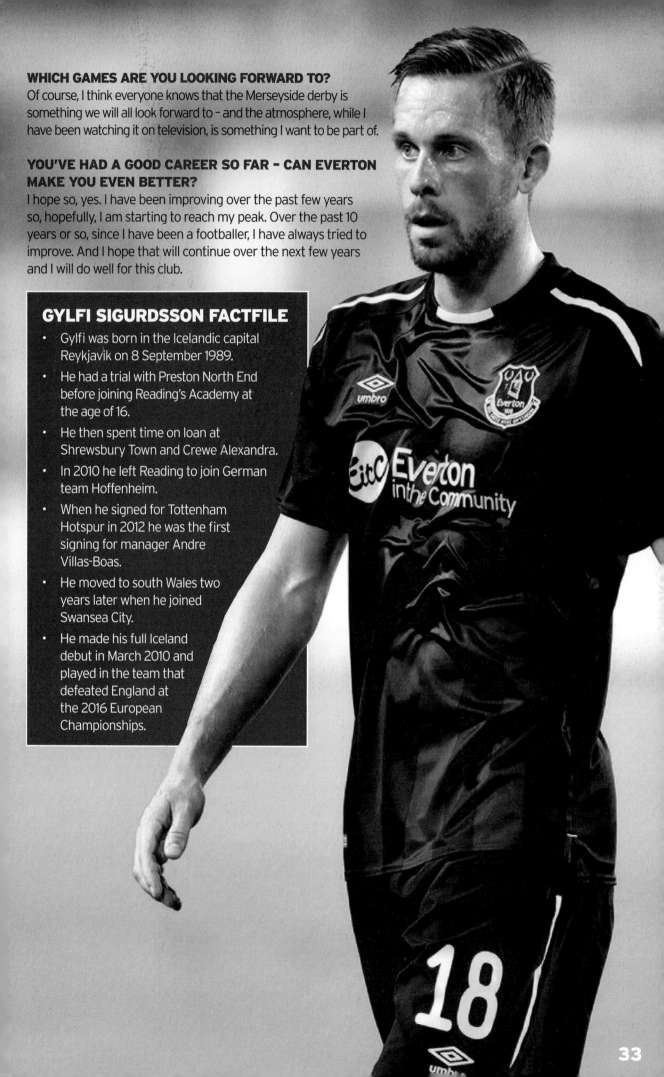

WHICH GAMES ARE YOU LOOKING FORWARD TO?
Of course, I think everyone knows that the Merseyside derby is something we will all look forward to - and the atmosphere, while I have been watching it on television, is something I want to be part of.

YOU'VE HAD A GOOD CAREER SO FAR - CAN EVERTON MAKE YOU EVEN BETTER?
I hope so, yes. I have been improving over the past few years so, hopefully, I am starting to reach my peak. Over the past 10 years or so, since I have been a footballer, I have always tried to improve. And I hope that will continue over the next few years and I will do well for this club.

GYLFI SIGURDSSON FACTFILE

- Gylfi was born in the Icelandic capital Reykjavik on 8 September 1989.

- He had a trial with Preston North End before joining Reading's Academy at the age of 16.

- He then spent time on loan at Shrewsbury Town and Crewe Alexandra.

- In 2010 he left Reading to join German team Hoffenheim.

- When he signed for Tottenham Hotspur in 2012 he was the first signing for manager Andre Villas-Boas.

- He moved to south Wales two years later when he joined Swansea City.

- He made his full Iceland debut in March 2010 and played in the team that defeated England at the 2016 European Championships.

SPOT THE DIFFERENCE

See if you can spot the six differences between these two Everton action shots.

Answers on p60-61

YOUR PREDICTIONS

Who'll win the Premier League? Who will be crowned Champions of Europe? Which country will be on top of the world in the summer? Who will win the FA Cup final at Wembley? It's up to you to decide!

Have a go at predicting the outcome of these competitions and ask your friends to do the same. Then, at the end of the season, get your EVERTON Annual off the shelf and see how many you got right!

COMPETITION	2016/17 WINNER	2018 WINNER
Premier League	Chelsea	
Championship	Newcastle United	
League One	Sheffield United	
League Two	Portsmouth	
FA Cup	Arsenal	
League Cup	Manchester United	
UEFA Champions League	Real Madrid	
Europa League	Manchester United	
World Cup	Germany (2010 winners)	
Premier League top scorer	Harry Kane	
Scottish Premier League	Celtic	
Everton's top goalscorer	Romelu Lukaku	

JUNIOR QUIZ

All these Premier League stars joined new clubs during the summer of 2017. All you need to do is name each player, the club they play for now and the club that sold them...

1 _____

2 _____

3 _____

4 _____

5 _____

6 _____

7 _____

8 _____

9 _____

10 _____

Answers on p60-61

NEW FOR 17-18

GET MORE EVERTON

JOIN TODAY

ADULTS £25

INTERNATIONALS† £25

YOUNG BLUES £10

INFANTS FREE

EXCLUSIVE CONTENT

WIN TICKETS

ONLINE CASHBACK

EVERTON GIFTS

AND MORE...

†The Internationals membership is priced at £25 regardless of age

PURCHASE ONLINE AT EVERTONFC.COM/GETMORE OR CALL 0151 556 1878

EVERTON IN AFRICA

Everton Football Club broke new ground during the summer of 2017 when we toured the east African country of Tanzania. We were the very first Premier League club to ever play a game in Tanzania and as you can see from our terrific photographs, we did far more than just play a football match.

For the record, we beat Kenyan champions Gor Mahia 2-1 in the Tanzanian national stadium, with goals from Wayne Rooney and Kieran Dowell, and while we were in Africa we really got out and about to meet the local people and sample a few traditional customs...

Idrissa Gueye meets children from a Deaf and Blind School in Dar es Salaam.

Kevin Mirallas and Morgan Schneiderlin get kitted out for a traditional dance.

Kevin Mirallas leads the way as the squad boards the flight from Liverpool to Dar es Salaam.

At a gala dinner, Her Excellency, the Vice President of Tanzania was delighted to meet Wayne Rooney.

Mo Besic and Michael Keane greet the players of Albino United.

Leon Osman takes the opportunity to play the drums in a Tanzanian village.

Wayne Rooney gets a souvenir of the trip.

The lads get the chance to taste the Tanzanian dishes that they cooked!

YOUR PHOTOS!

We asked you to send us your favourite photos of you supporting the Blues...!

DESIGN YOUR OWN EVERTON CHRISTMAS JUMPER!

The players wear them and so do the fans. They are as much a part of the festive season as mistletoe, turkey, wrapping paper and mince pies! Christmas Jumpers! Use this page to design your own Everton Christmas Jumper...

WORDSEARCH

Hidden within this grid are ten Premier League players. See if you can find them all and give yourself three minutes to do so...

Aguero
Antonio
Benteke
Deeney
Hazard
Kane
Pickford
Pogba
Vardy
Walcott

O	I	N	O	T	N	A	E	J	V
M	A	T	L	M	R	B	N	W	N
N	H	B	W	Q	E	Y	A	A	P
Y	V	P	G	N	H	G	K	L	I
E	R	A	T	O	D	J	B	C	C
N	T	E	R	R	P	C	B	O	K
E	K	R	A	D	V	B	Z	T	F
E	K	Z	H	W	Y	T	T	T	O
D	A	A	G	U	E	R	O	K	R
H	H	K	N	Q	P	R	Q	Z	D

Answers on p60-61

43

DIXIE DEAN

The 1927/28 season was one of the most amazing campaigns in the history of English football. Everton ended the season as the First Division Champions but even that feat was over-shadowed by the greatest centre-forward who ever played the game.

William Ralph 'Dixie' Dean was a goals machine who had joined Everton from Tranmere Rovers in 1926. His tally of 383 Everton goals will probably last forever and so will his achievement in 1927/28...

When George Camsell scored 59 Football League goals for Middlesbrough in 1926/27 he must have believed that his record would never, ever be beaten. But it was. In fact, it only lasted for one season before being bettered by Dixie Dean.

Amazingly, Dean was only 20 years of age when the 1927/28 kicked-off and he started in terrific form,

scoring in every one of the opening nine games – bagging 17 goals in the process, including all five in a 5-2 win against Manchester United in October!

By Christmas his total had motored on to 31 goals and people started to wonder whether he would break the record. He continued to score regularly in the new year but with seven matches of the season remaining he still needed 15 to reach the magical figure of 60.

When there were just three games left he was on 51 goals. Some people thought that he had given

60

LEAGUE GOALS IN ONE SEASON

sixth minute Dean was fouled in the box and duly converted the penalty kick. The record was equalled and the great man had plenty of time to beat it.

However, time ebbed away and with eight minutes to go, Dean was still stuck on 59 goals. The crowd was getting very anxious. Surely their man wasn't going to get so far only to fail to create history? Then Alec Troup sent a corner-kick into the penalty area and Dean climbed higher than the Arsenal defence to power a header past the goalkeeper and into the net. Goodison Park erupted and it took the referee a good few minutes to restore order and restart the game. Dean actually left the field before the final whistle so he wouldn't get mobbed again at the end of the match!

60 league goals in one season – and Dean missed three of the games, including a 7-0 win against West Ham so his incredible tally could have been even more!

himself too much to do and against Aston Villa on 21 April he only netted twice in a 3-2 victory at Goodison.

Two games left, seven goals needed. It was a massive task, even for a goalscorer like Dixie Dean. The last away game of the season was at Turf Moor against Burnley and Dean scored in the very first minute. By half-time he had scored another hat-trick and he found the net again in the second half for a four-goal haul in a 5-2 win.

So, it all came down to the last game and the maths was simple. Dixie Dean needed to score yet another hat-trick to break a record that everybody thought was unbreakable.

It was Saturday 5 May 1927 and 48,715 Evertonians were at Goodison to welcome the newly-crowned League champions and, just as importantly, to see if Dean could get the goals he needed to take Camsell's record. The visitors, Arsenal, opened the scoring after just two minutes but Dean equalised a minute later. The blistering start to the game continued and in the

EVERTON LADIES

THE EVERTON LADIES FOOTY TEAM IS BACK IN THE TOP DIVISION THIS SEASON AND MANAGER ANDY SPENCE IS DELIGHTED...

How excited are you for Everton Ladies to be back in WSL1 this season?

Very! It's obviously the best league for us to be in and we've got good and exciting young players in this team who want to test themselves at the highest level and that's what we're doing!

The team went fully professional before the season started. What was that like?

Busy! It's always a busy time in the off-season but we really were working every day to bring players in who could help us. Our general manager was in Venice at one stage signing a player on a gondola! So it was exciting as well and we were lucky that we were able to target players who we really wanted and maybe weren't able to get before.

There were lots of new faces but, like the men's team, Everton Ladies like to bring their own young players through as well...

We absolutely do. That will always be important to us and we've got five girls who came right through our academy set-up and others who have been with us from the age of 16 or 17. We'll always invest in our young ones because they help to bring a bit of Scouse bite to our team!

The girls train full-time at Finch Farm now. How much have they enjoyed training alongside Ronald Koeman and his team?

It's been a huge inspiration. It's a brilliant facility which we've always been able to use but it had to be evenings because the players were working in the day. Now we're here every day, training alongside the young lads in the Academy and the first team and that can only be good for our players. We very much feel like part of the Everton family!

What advice would you give to somebody who wanted to pursue a career in women's football?

Just go for it! A young girl can dream of growing up to be a professional footballer because the opportunity is there now and that's brilliant. Young

Follow Everton Ladies at everton.fawsl.com or search 'Everton Ladies' on social media

girls can look up to the likes of Gabby George, Claudia Walker, Dan Turner and Georgia Brougham, girls who had a tough journey to get where they are today. That said, to make it to the top you will always need to work hard, be dedicated and really put your heart and soul into your football.

And what if you want to play for Everton? What do you need to do?

First and foremost, play football as much as possible - whether that's at school, with friends or at a local club. I always say it's important to fall in love with the game and then stay in love with it. Every year, we open up the doors of the club for trials and anyone can apply to take part in those. Just look out for information on our website!

EVERTON IN THE COMMUNITY

The official charity of Everton Football Club helps thousands of people from all over Merseyside every year and has the reputation of being the best in the Premier League.

Since 1988, Everton in the Community has been helping people, young and old, from many different backgrounds in lots of ways including health, education and helping people into employment.

The charity works with children and adults to teach them about the benefits of eating healthily and doing regular exercise and also helps people find new jobs and gain qualifications.

A few nights a week, the charity runs a programme called **Kicks** which gives young people from all over Liverpool a safe place to play sports and keep them off the streets and out of trouble and the **Safe Hands** programme helps young adults who have been in trouble with the police get their lives back on track.

The Premier League provides funding for many of the programmes that Everton in the Community deliver and one of the most popular is **Premier League 4 Sport**, which gives school children the opportunity to try sports that they may not have tried before like judo, table tennis and hockey.

But it's not just young people who benefit from the many initiatives hosted by the charity. Everton in the Community is regularly praised for the work it does with ex-soldiers and people who struggle with mental health issues. Older people aren't forgotten about either. The programme, **Stand Together**, helps those who are experiencing loneliness.

Everton even became the first Premier League football club to have its own **Free School** which is

Gareth Barry joins the fun at a Kicks session

David Unsworth and his players say 'thanks' after the 'Home Is Where The Heart Is' initiative reaches its target

THANK YOU

Ronald Koeman puts a sprint on duing an EitC visit

open to young people aged 14-19 and provides exciting learning opportunities in a fantastic new building which is on Spellow Lane, just a goal-kick from Goodison Park.

There was much excitement in 2017, the charity's new home **'The People's Hub'** was officially opened by HRH Prince Edward, The Earl of Wessex whilst Blues boss Ronald Koeman declared the **Cruyff Court Everton** 'open' when he took part in a penalty shootout with some local school children. Based at The People's Hub, Cruyff Court Everton is a community facility that provides children in the local neighbourhood with a safe place to play sports and is part-funded by the Johan Cruyff Foundation, after the famous Dutch footballer.

Throughout the season, the players visit lots of Everton in the Community programmes to find out more about the great work they do and to meet the people that the charity helps. Sometimes they get involved with classroom or sports sessions with children and other times they spend time playing games with old people or presenting trophies to players at the charity's annual Disability Awards Ceremony.

At Christmas, the entire first-team squad visit the sick children at Alder Hey Children's Hospital and deliver presents to help put smiles on the faces of them and their families...and of course the doctors and nurses!

The work that Everton in the Community does is recognised by people all over the world and in the last five years they have received over 100 awards for its brilliant work in helping others.

Everton in the Community also has a number of high-profile ambassadors and patrons who work to raise awareness of the charity's work, including Britain's Got Talent judge Amanda Holden and award-winning actress Dame Judi Dench.

This year Everton Under-23 manager David Unsworth and his Premier League 2 winning squad fundraised over £230,000 to support homeless people sleeping on the streets of Liverpool and even slept out at Goodison Park on a freezing cold night in November to experience homelessness for themselves.

The charity also fundraises throughout the year to raise money to help them continue their impressive work and there are lots of different ways that fans can get involved to help. Some fans have done a skydive, abseiled down Liverpool Cathedral and taken part in the annual EitC golf day whilst local schools have held sponsored silences and cake stalls to help the charity of their favourite club.

Phil Jagielka at an EitC session at Goodison Park

Tom Davies with a pupil at the Free School

Ronald Koeman tees off at the EitC Golf Day

@EitC
community.evertonfc.com

Leighton Baines tries his hand at graffiti

Ian Snodin and Seamus Coleman pose for a team photo with some of the Everton Downs Syndrome players

@EitC
community.evertonfc.com

Everton Community

PLAY LIKE YOUR HEROES

For the best time with a football outside of Goodison Park, why not sign your child up for an Everton Soccer School?

Children will be taught the skills and techniques that have kept Premier League stars such as Wayne Rooney, Leighton Baines and Tom Davies and at the top of their game.

Everton Soccer Schools typically take place throughout Merseyside and North Wales.
Prices start at £10 per day.

WWW.EVERTONFC.COM/SOCCERSCHOOLS

POSTER POWER
LEIGHTON BAINES
10 YEARS A BLUE

DAVY
KLAASSEN'S
SOCCER TIPS

Dutch team Ajax Amsterdam are famous for producing clever, skilful footballers. They have been European champions four times and many of their former players have become global stars. So when Everton signed Davy Klaassen from Ajax in the summer, fans were understandably excited at the thought of having their own Holland international running out at Goodison Park. Davy is 5ft 10.5in – small compared to some Premier league footballers – but he makes up for this with his sparkling feet and intelligent play! Here, the 24-year-old reveals how he has made himself one of the most talked about attacking players in Europe...

Davy on his favourite position...

"One season at Ajax, I played as a holding midfielder for a few months. I prefer to play in a more attacking position, I think I can be more important there than when I am deeper. It is different when you play further forward – the angles are different and the runs you have to make are different."

Davy on the most valuable lesson he learned at Ajax...

"First touch is one of the most important things in football. Every touch you take uses one or two extra seconds. When you play first touch, you speed up your game. When your first touch is good, you save yourself extra time and you can make the right decision. That is what I have learned in the past 10 years."

Davy on linking up with his teammates...

"We look to each other – I see what the other player likes, then I can make my run. I like it when the striker drops deeper on the pitch, then I can run into the space he has left behind him."

Davy on looking after himself...

"I have to be fit... when I do not feel really fit, it is difficult to play well. I played every single game for the past four years. When you keep playing, your stamina is good. The games are the best training!"

Davy on the best-ever Premier League players in his position: Paul Scholes and Frank Lampard...

"Hopefully, I can get to their level. I am still young. I will try my best and we will see. Being smaller does not matter. It is more about fast thinking. The more you see, the faster you can play – and that is important!"

WORLD CUP QUIZ

You won't need to worry about being bored next summer because you'll be able to watch the 2018 World Cup! The tournament is being staged in Russia and we can't wait for it to start! See how much you know about the biggest footy competition of them all with our special 'World Cup Quiz'.

Answers on p60-61

1. Where was the last World Cup played in 2014?

....

2. Who were the winners?

....

3. Which country famously lost 7-1 in the semi-finals?

4. Which current Premier League player was voted as the Best Young Player of the 2014 tournament? Was it Paul Pogba (France), Sergio Aguero (Argentina) or Kevin De Bruyne (Belgium)?

....

5. England were in a group with Uruguay, Italy and Costa Rica - how many games did they win?

....

6. The original World Cup trophy was named after which person - Stanley Rous or Jules Rimet?

....

7. Which country got to keep the original trophy forever after winning it three times?

....

8. In what year did England win the competition?

Italy were the champions in 1982, beating West Germany in the final

9. Who did we beat in the final?

10. Who was the only Everton player in the England team that won the final - Ray Wilson or Alan Ball?

11. How many times did the great Pele win the World Cup with Brazil? 1,2 or 3 times?

12. Which country hosted and won the very first World Cup tournament in 1930?

13. The only England player to ever be a World Cup top scorer was Bobby Charlton, Gary Lineker or Alan Shearer?

Brazil won the tournament for a record fifth time in 2002

Germany won the 1990 final after beating England in the semi-final

14. Where will the 2022 World Cup finals be held? Saudi Arabia, USA or Qatar?

15. Who has won the most World Cups between Argentina and Spain?

16. All these countries have staged a World Cup finals tournament. We've mixed up the letters of each nation and all you have to do is figure out the names of the countries...

a. COXEMI

b. CAMECIR

c. GLENDAN

d. GREATNIAN

e. LAYTI

f. GRAYMEN

g. CARFEN

h. ASPIN

i. DEWSEN

j. DEWSRITZNAL

WORLD CUP BLUES

Everton Football Club has provided players for eleven of the twenty World Cup finals that have been staged since the first tournament way back in 1930.

Only one man has ever won the World Cup whilst with Everton and that was Ray Wilson, who was England's left-back in the 1966 final at Wembley against West Germany. Alan Ball was also in the team that day but he was still a Blackpool player and didn't join the Blues until after the final.

In South Africa in 2010, John Heitinga almost became the second Everton player to secure a World Cup winners medal but his Holland team lost in the final against Spain. Indeed, Heitinga's disappointment was compounded by the fact that he was sent-off in the final.

Two players have reached a World Cup semi-final whilst with Everton. In 1998 in France, Croatia surprised many experts when they reached the last four and part of their team was Toffees centre-half Slaven Bilic. The Croats lost to France in the last four and after a Premier League season that saw Everton avoid relegation only on goal difference, it was hardly surprising that Bilic was our only representative at that World Cup.

Blues legend Brian Labone (far left) in action against West Germany in the 1970 quarter-final.

Then in 2006, when the Word Cup finals were staged in Germany, Everton left-back Nuno Valente went all the way through to the semi-finals with Portugal, where they lost narrowly to France. Valente had been part of the Portuguese side that defeated England on penalties in the quarter-final.

That's not the only time that an Everton player has appeared against England in a World Cup finals

Everton were well represented in Mexico in 1986 with four players in this England line-up – Peter Reid, Gary Lineker, Trevor Steven and Gary Stevens.

competition. The first occurrence was in 1990, in Italy, when Kevin Sheedy played for the Republic of Ireland against Bobby Robson's England. Sheedy scored the goal, Ireland's first World Cup finals goal ever, in a 1-1 draw and he is still the only Everton to player to find the net against England in a World Cup finals game.

The others to play against England are Niclas Alexandersson and Tobias Linderoth for Sweden in 2002, Thomas Gravesen for Denmark in the same tournament, and Tim Howard for USA in 2010.

In 2014, Howard was involved in the only World Cup finals match that has ever featured an Everton player on BOTH sides when he opposed Kevin Mirallas in the USA's narrow defeat to Belgium (Romelu Lukaku also played but he was still technically a Chelsea player at the time).

The most players that Everton have provided in one game at any World Cup finals was in 1986 when we had FOUR men in the England side. Gary Lineker, Peter Reid, Gary Stevens and Trevor Steven all played in wins against Poland and Paraguay and then the quarter-final defeat against Argentina.

Lineker was the tournament's top goalscorer in 1986 with six - the only time an Everton player has ever won the World Cup Golden Boot.

Somewhat surprisingly, apart from those six Lineker goals, Everton have only provided two other World Cup finals goalscorers. Stuart McCall scored one for Scotland in 1990 and then Tim Cahill netted twice for Australia in 2006 and another one in 2010.

Indeed, Cahill's goal in 2006 against Japan was the first ever Australia goal in a World cup finals tournament.

Hopefully, we'll add to that tally in Russia in the summer of 2018...

John Heitinga became the second Everton player to appear in a World Cup final in 2010 but he was sent off before the end!

Everton's Kevin Mirallas is denied by his team-mate Tim Howard during the 2014 World Cup.

Gary Lineker celebrates another goal in Mexico.

Ray Wilson is still the only player to win the World Cup whilst with Everton.

GOODISON MATCHDAY

There's nothing quite like Goodison Park on a matchday! In 2017, the Blues home celebrates its 125th birthday, having been built in 1892. It remains one of the most popular and traditional footy grounds in the country and this is what happens when Everton play at home...

The groundstaff are out very early on a matchday to give the pitch a final cut before the game.

The white lines have to be perfectly straight... especially the ones in the penalty area!

Good pals on and off the pitch, Tom Davies and Mason Holgate often travel to the games together.

Wayne Rooney always likes to arrive in plenty of time before the match.

Once inside the stadium the players will walk up the corridor towards the dressing room...

...where the kit will be waiting for them.

Meanwhile, back outside the sign in Bullens Road tells the away fans where they need to go...

...as Evertonians of all ages arrive at Goodison Park hoping to see their team win.

Two large police horses make their way through the crowd before the game.

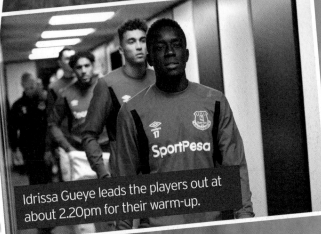

Idrissa Gueye leads the players out at about 2.20pm for their warm-up.

Then at 2.55pm, Phil Jagielka is at the head of the line as the two teams wait for Z-Cars to play.

...and this is their view!

Nearly time for kick-off! The players walk out to greet the supporters.

The game is over, the job is done and Ronald Koeman tells the media what he thought of Everton's performance.

QUIZ ANSWERS

P11: WAYNE ROONEY QUIZ

1) A. Alan Shearer

2) B. Manchester City

3) B. Aston Villa

4) C. Sven-Goran Eriksson

5) C. Four

P24: INTERNATIONAL BLUES!

Belgium – Kevin Mirallas

Bosnia – Muhamed Besic

England – Ross Barkley

France – Morgan Schneiderlin

Holland – Davy Klaassen

Republic of Ireland – Seamus Coleman

Spain – Sandro Ramirez

Wales – Ashley Williams

Iceland – Gylfi Sigurdsson

P20 WORDSEARCH

O	I	N	O	T	N	A	E	J	V
M	A	T	L	M	R	B	N	W	N
N	H	B	W	Q	E	Y	A	A	P
Y	V	P	G	N	H	G	K	L	I
E	R	A	T	O	D	J	B	C	C
N	T	E	R	R	P	C	B	O	K
E	K	R	A	D	V	B	Z	T	F
E	K	Z	H	W	Y	T	T	T	O
D	A	A	G	U	E	R	O	K	R
H	H	K	N	Q	P	R	Q	Z	D

P34: SPOT THE DIFFERENCE

P30: OLD STADIUM QUIZ

Stadium A. Coventry City, Highfield Road

Stadium B. Manchester City, Maine Road

Stadium C. Leicester City, Filbert Street

Stadium D. Shrewsbury Town, Gay Meadow

Stadium E. Sunderland, Roker Park

Stadium F. Arsenal, Highbury

Stadium G. West Ham United, Upton Park

Stadium H. Wimbedon, Plough Lane

Stadium I. Southampton, The Dell

P36: JUNIOR QUIZ

1. Nemanja Matic, Chelsea to Manchester United

2. Kyle Walker, Tottenham Hotspur to Manchester City

3. Alexandre Lacazette, Lyon to Arsenal

4. Pablo Zabaleta, Manchester City to West Ham

5. Jonathan Walters, Stoke City to Burnley

6. Neymar, Barcelona to Paris St Germain

7. Gareth Barry, Everton to West Brom

8. Andre Gray, Burnley to Watford

9. Kelechi Iheanacho, Manchester City to Leicester City

10. Javier Hernandez, Bayer Leverkusen to West Ham

P54/55: WORLD CUP QUIZ

1) Brazil

2) Germany

3) Brazil

4) Paul Pogba

5) None!

6) Jules Rimet

7) Brazil

8) 1966

9) West Germany

10) Ray Wilson

11) 3

12) Uruguay

13) Gary Lineker in 1986

14) Qatar

15) Argentina

16)   a) Mexico 1970 & 1986
       b) America 1994
       c) England 1966
       d) Argentina 1978
       e) Italy 1934 & 1990
       f) Germany 1974 & 2002
       g) France 1938 & 1998
       h) Spain 1982
       i) Sweden 1958
       j) Switzerland 1934